THE GREATEST FISH I EVER CAUGHT

"I caught a 5-pound bass on my 5th birthday"

WORKBOOK PRESS
RECOMMENDED
LITERARY BOOK COMPETITION 2021

DENNIS MEADOWS

WORKBOOK PRESS LLC
187 E Warm Springs Rd,
Suite B285, Las Vegas, NV 89119, USA

Website: https://workbookpress.com/
Hotline: 1-888-818-4856
Email: admin@workbookpress.com

Ordering Information:
Quantity sales. Special discounts are available on quantity purchases by corporations, associations, and others.
For details, contact the publisher at the address above.

ISBN-13:   978-1-956876-02-4 (Paperback Version)
                  978-1-956876-03-1 (Digital Version)

REV. DATE: 05/11/2021

Greatest Fish I Ever Caught

Dennis Meadows

As a child, my dad went hunting and fishing a lot even when he was alone. He usually always brought some fish home. One day, I asked him to take me, and he said he would. Well, I think he was busy working on the old car we had, I guess. It seems about after two or three weeks of begging him that he took me.

It was on my fifth birthday, and I think it was Saturday, but not sure. I was very excited as we got started. It was my first fishing trip, and I was very happy to start the day.

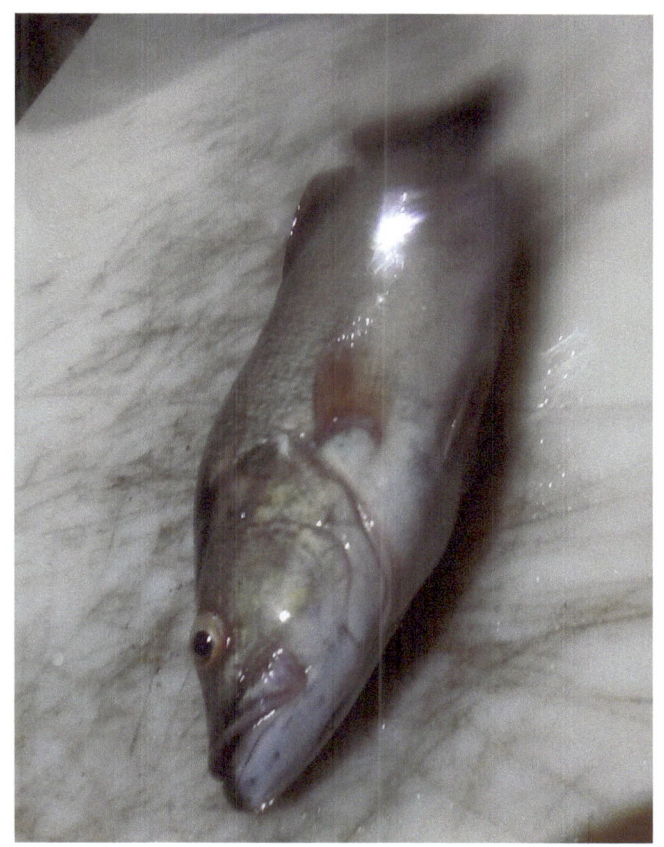

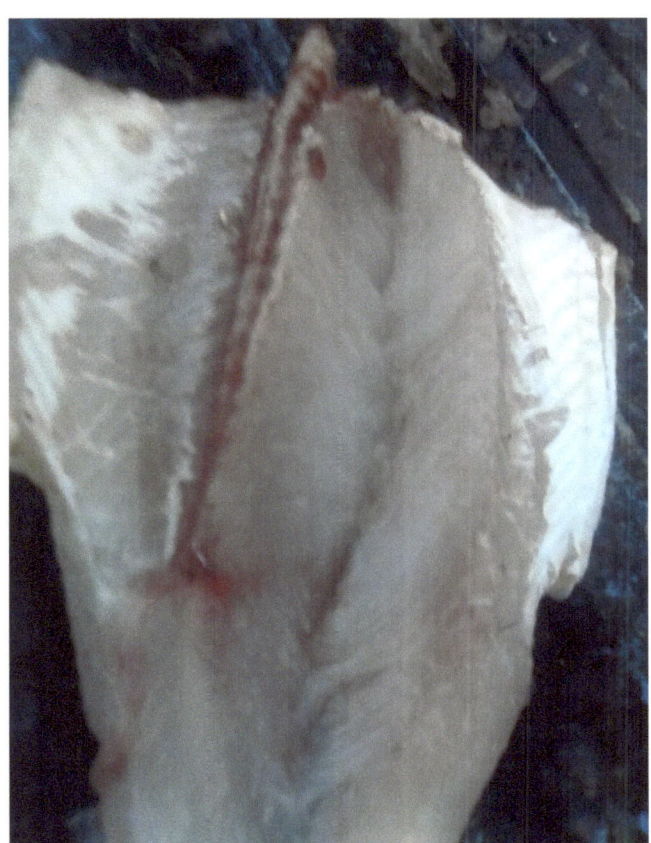

In Genesis 1:26, God said, "Let us make man in our image, after our likeness, and let them have dominion over the fish of the sea." God was about to prove it that day. We got up and got the fishing gear in the car.

It was summertime, and I think it was about seven in the morning when we got there after about thirty minutes of driving. The grass was high, about eight or ten inches, and the brown weeds were higher. It had a little path not very much used. We walked some little ways because I remember I was tired, since it was about eighth or quarter of a mile.

It was a river, and it was kind of deep. The place where we stopped had a little place where I could sit in front of my dad. Really, I think I was using a cane pole. We were using worms, and he put it on the hook for me. It wasn't very long about ten minutes, I guess. All of a sudden, a big five-pound bass took the worm and hook. My dad, helped me bring the big fish in and I was so excited! At the time, I thought it would be the greatest fish I ever caught but it was not. We then packed up and went home.

As I got older, I took a fishing trip at my aunt and uncle's house. It seems I was running from God, and I went there for several days. My uncle Reece took me on a crab fishing trip for the very first time. He bought some chicken necks, and cut some little poles about four feet long. We got into his car and rode about thirty minutes, and suddenly, he pulled over by a ditch. We got out, and he had two or three five-gallon buckets.

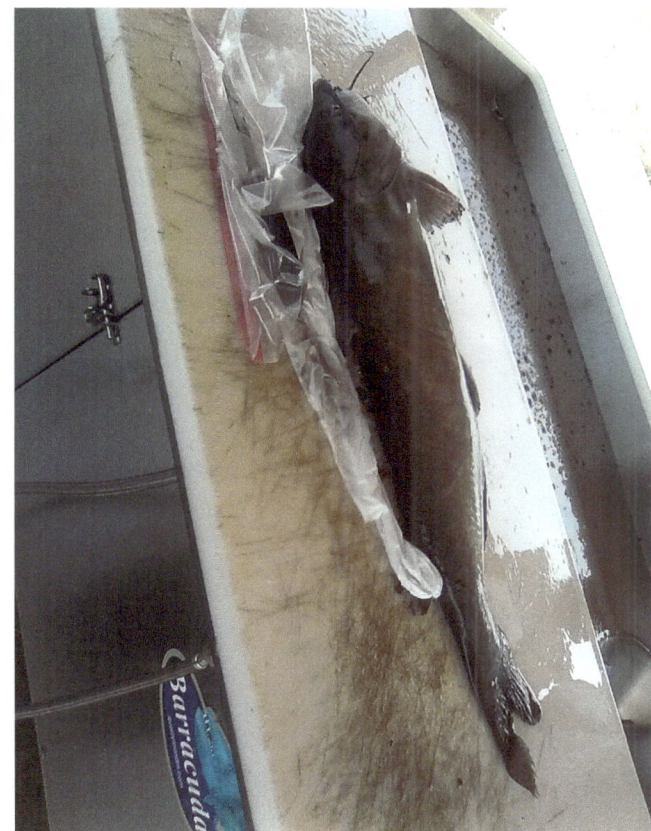

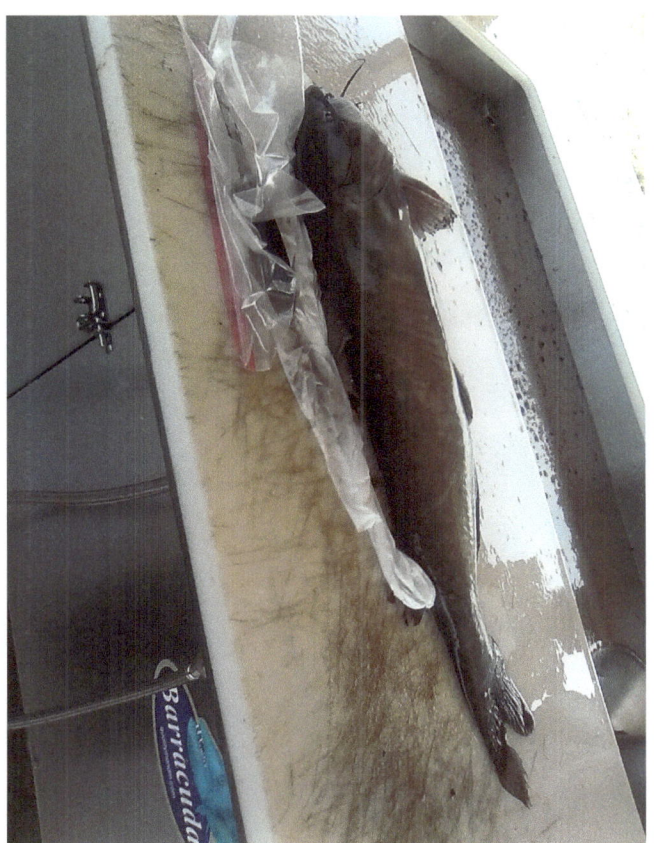

The ditch had water in it, and it was maybe five or six feet across, but it was pretty cheap. Well, he took one of the chicken necks, and put one on the hook. It was really fast when a crab jumped up and grabbed it and took it under the water.

My eyes got big because I had never seen anything like that before. After we had three five-gallon buckets full we left. We went to their home, and he got a big pan out and cooked them. He gave me some sauce, and we ate until we are full.

That was a fishing trip for crabs. In Luke 5:10, Jesus said to Simon, "Fear not, from henceforth thou shall catch men." I didn't know it at the time, but God was about to make me a fisher of men!

It was a day later or so that I was to catch the greatest fish I ever caught. It was a normal day on about July 7th. When I woke up that day, about 10 am, the sun was shining brightly. When I walked outside, I saw three calves out in the field. I crawled up onto the hog pen, and sat on the roof while I enjoyed looking around at the scenery. As I sat there thinking, the Holy Spirit came upon me greatly. A bible verse came to my mind from the gospel of John 14, "I am the Way, the Truth, and the Life. No man can come to Father but by Me."

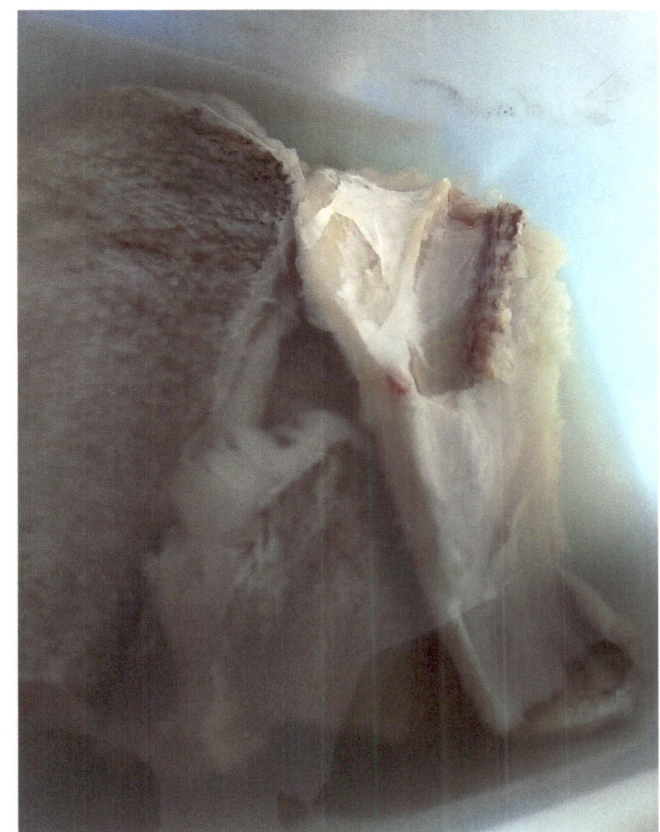

Our enemy told me not to listen, but tried to show me the whole world. I bowed my head, and wept as I asked Jesus to come into my heart. I felt a great burden leave my body, as the Holy Spirit came into my soul. He told me it would be my last chance to be saved.

It was God's Word that was used to catch the greatest fish I ever caught. It was His Son, Jesus Christ, and still is today.

For over two hours after that, the Holy Spirit was greatly upon me. The birds were singing, and the snake was gone forever. I am sure that a poisonous snake was close to me that day, but God stopped it from biting me. God's Holy Spirit helped me to say yes, and I am glad it did. Otherwise, I would forever be in hell. Forever and ever!

As I have caught many fish since then, I use real bait, because I catch more. God used his Son and He is the only one that can make you live forever.